Lacy Sunshine
Love Note Fairies and Angel Kisses
Coloring Book Volume 29

Illustrated by
Heather Valentin

©Heather Valentin. Lacy Sunshine. All Rights Reserved.
No redistribution without artist's permission.

This book belongs to

Made in the USA
Middletown, DE
20 May 2018